T___

RECIPES

Traditional Cakes
from the Emerald Isle

*With scenes from
Old Irish Life*

by

Francis S. Walker R.H.A.

SALMON

Index

Title page picture: A Woman's Task

Irish Whiskey Cake

A fruit cake enticingly flavoured with whiskey and orange.

1 orange	6 oz. caster sugar
2 tablespoons Irish whiskey	3 eggs, beaten
6 oz. sultanas	8 oz. flour
6 oz. butter	1 teaspoon baking powder

Pinch of salt

Peel the orange thinly and place the peel in a bowl with 1 teaspoon of squeezed orange juice. Stir in the whiskey and sultanas, cover and leave in a cool place overnight. Next morning, remove the orange peel and discard. Set oven to 350ºF or Mark 4. Cream the butter and sugar together in a bowl until fluffy, then add the beaten eggs, a little at a time. Sift the flour, baking powder and salt together and fold into the mixture, then stir in the orange, whiskey and fruit mixture. Turn into a greased and lined 7 inch cake tin and bake for 1 to $1\frac{1}{4}$ hours, covering the top with kitchen foil if it appears to be browning too quickly. Cool in the tin for at least 10 minutes, then turn out on to a wire rack.

If desired, a little icing, made with sifted icing sugar combined with orange juice, can be drizzled over the top of the cake when it is completely cold.

A Country Fair

Barm Brack

Although Barm Brack or 'speckled bread' is usually made with a yeasted dough, there are other delicious unyeasted versions; in this one the fruit is soaked in tea.

6oz. soft brown sugar	**¾ pint freshly made tea (no milk)**
5 oz. sultanas or currants	**1 egg, beaten**
5 oz. raisins	**12 oz. self-raising flour**
2 oz. chopped mixed peel	**1 teaspoon mixed spice**

A little warmed honey

Put the sugar, fruit and peel in a bowl, pour over the tea, cover and leave to stand overnight. Set oven to 350°F or Mark 4. Stir the beaten egg into the fruit mixture, then sift in the flour and spice and combine thoroughly. Turn into a greased and base-lined 2 lb. loaf tin, smooth over the top and bake for 1 to 1¼ hours until well risen and firm to the touch, covering the top with kitchen foil if it appears to be browning too quickly. Five minutes before the end of baking time, glaze the top with warmed honey and return to the oven to finish cooking. Cool in the tin for 5 minutes, then turn out on to a wire rack. Serve sliced with butter.

This Barm Brack is moist and a good 'keeper'; it also freezes well. As, traditionally, Barm Brack is round in shape it can, if preferred, be baked in a greased and base-lined 9 inch round cake tin.

Potato Scones

These quickly made scones were traditionally baked on a griddle or bakestone and served hot at breakfast or tea.

8 oz. cold, well-mashed potatoes   ½ **teaspoon salt**
½ **oz. melted butter**   **2 oz. flour**
½ **teaspoon baking powder**

Combine the potatoes, butter and salt thoroughly together in a bowl. Sift the flour and baking powder together, then stir into the potatoes to form a pliable dough. Turn out on to a lightly floured surface and roll out. Using a tea plate as a guide, cut round to form the dough into 2 or 3 circles, then cut each circle into quarters and prick with a fork. Heat a buttered frying pan and cook for 5 to 6 minutes, turning once. Serve hot with butter.

Cherry Dog

The classic Cherry Cake is as popular in Ireland as it is in mainland Britain, but Cherry Dog is an Irish variation which was an appetising and practical way to use up any left-over dough from a baking or breadmaking session.

3 oz. glacé cherries	Pinch of salt
8 oz. flour	2 oz. butter
2 level teaspoons cream of tartar	2 oz. sugar
1 level teaspoon bicarbonate of soda	1 egg, beaten
	Milk

A little extra sugar for sprinkling

Set oven to 400°F or Mark 6. Cut the cherries into halves or quarters, rinse in warm water to remove any excess syrup, dry thoroughly and toss in a little flour. Sift together into a bowl the flour, cream of tartar, bicarbonate of soda and salt, rub in the butter until the mixture resembles breadcrumbs, then stir in the sugar and the prepared cherries. Make a well in the centre of the dry mixture, drop in the egg and gradually work in the dry mixture from the sides, adding sufficient milk to produce a smooth, elastic dough. Turn out on to a lightly floured surface, knead lightly and then, with the hands, form into a round or into a thick sausage shape. Place on a greased baking sheet, brush with milk to glaze then sprinkle with a little sugar. Bake for about 30 minutes, until golden. Cool on a wire rack and serve plain or spread with butter.

Ballywindland Rolls

These sweet, teatime rolls, more pastry than scones or yeasted rolls, are prepared in the same way as rough-puff pastry.

1 lb. flour
2 teaspoons baking powder
Pinch of salt

5 oz. softened butter,
cut into small cubes
Milk, sweetened with a little sugar

Milk or egg mixed with milk, to glaze

Sift together into a bowl the flour, baking powder and salt, lightly rub in the butter then add sufficient sweetened milk to form an elastic dough. Turn out on to a lightly floured surface and shape into a square. Roll into an oblong, fold into three by folding down the top third and then folding up the bottom third to cover it. Seal the edges, give a quarter turn and roll out. Allow to rest in a cool place for 10 minutes, then repeat the folding, rolling and resting process twice more. Set oven to 400°F or Mark 6. Cut the dough into rounds, brush lightly with milk and fold over to form half-circles, sealing well. Place on a lightly greased baking sheet, glaze with milk or egg and milk and bake for 20 minutes until golden brown. Cool on a wire rack. Serve plain or with honey.

The Piper's Visit

Chocolate Sandwich Cake

This cake, with its filling of whipped cream, contains mashed potato, that popular ingredient in Irish cooking.

4 oz. butter, softened	2 eggs, beaten
6 oz. caster sugar	6 oz. self-raising flour
3 oz. finely mashed potatoes	Milk
2 oz. plain chocolate, melted	Whipped cream

A little sifted icing sugar for sprinkling

Set oven to 350°F or Mark 4. Cream the butter, sugar and mashed potato together in a bowl until fluffy, then stir in the chocolate, melted in a bowl set over a pan of hot water. Whisk in the eggs, then fold in the flour and add sufficient milk to produce a soft, dropping consistency. Turn into two greased and base-lined 8 inch sandwich tins, smooth over the tops and bake for 25 to 30 minutes, until springy to the touch. Cool on a wire rack and, when cold, sandwich together with whipped cream and sprinkle the top with a little sifted icing sugar.

If desired, $1\frac{1}{2}$ to 2 oz. of sifted cocoa powder can be substituted for the melted chocolate.

Buttermilk Pancakes

Traditionally served at teatime spread with honey, these griddle-cooked
pancakes have always been favourites with children.

8 oz. flour	**2 eggs, beaten**
¹/₂ teaspoon salt	**Buttermilk**
¹/₂ teaspoon bicarbonate of soda	

Sift together into a bowl the flour, salt and bicarbonate of soda and beat in the eggs and sufficient buttermilk to make a fairly thick batter. Heat a well-buttered griddle or heavy frying pan, drop on to it tablespoons of the batter and cook for 3 to 4 minutes, turning once, until golden. Serve warm with honey or jam.

If desired, these pancakes can be made with fresh full-cream milk.

A Happy House

Saint Patrick's Cakes

Named after the patron saint of Ireland, these little iced sponge cakes were traditionally baked in three-cornered tins to represent shamrocks.

4 oz. butter	4 oz. flour
4 oz. caster sugar	1 teaspoon baking powder
2 eggs	White glacé icing

A little green food colouring

Set oven to 375°F or Mark 5. Cream the butter and sugar together in a bowl until fluffy. Beat the eggs in a bowl set over a pan of warm water, then stir into the butter mixture a little at a time. Sift the flour and baking powder together and fold in. Place about 12 paper cake cases into tartlet tins and divide the mixture between them. Bake for about 15 minutes or until the cakes are well risen and golden. Cool on a wire rack. Reserving a little of the icing, coat the cakes with the remainder and allow to set. Colour the reserved icing green, place in an icing bag with a plain piping nozzle attached and pipe a small shamrock in the centre of each cake.

Saffron Cake

In the 18th century, saffron - the dried stamens of the Saffron Crocus - was imported into Ireland from Cornwall. It was intended, primarily, as a yellow dye for tweed, but it also found its way into the kitchen, where it was used in baking.

½ **pint milk**	**Pinch of ground mace**
½ **teaspoon saffron threads**	**3 oz. sugar**
¼ **oz. dried yeast**	**6 oz. butter**
1 lb. strong flour	**2 oz. chopped mixed peel**
1 teaspoon salt	**6 oz. currants**

Bring the milk to the boil in a pan, stir in the saffron threads and leave to stand for 30 to 40 minutes. Strain, reheat the milk until tepid, add the yeast and leave until the mixture foams. Sift together into a bowl the flour, salt and mace, stir in the sugar and rub in the butter until the mixture resembles breadcrumbs. Stir in the yeast mixture and work in to a soft dough. Add the peel and dried fruit, cover with a clean tea-towel and leave in a warm place to rise for about 1 hour. Turn the dough out on to a lightly floured surface, knead for 2 to 3 minutes, place in a greased 8 inch cake tin and leave to stand for 15 minutes. Set oven to 350°F or Mark 4. Bake for 1 hour, covering the top with kitchen foil if it appears to be browning too quickly. Cool in the tin and serve sliced, plain, or spread with butter. If desired, Saffron Cake can be glazed with a little warm honey as it comes out of the oven.

Pratie Oaten

'Pratie' is slang for potato in Ireland and these potato oatcakes are a popular teatime treat in County Antrim.

1 lb. cooked, well-mashed potatoes	**Salt and pepper**
8 oz. fine oatmeal	**Milk**

Mix the potatoes, oatmeal and seasoning well together in a bowl, then add sufficient milk to form a soft, dough-like consistency. Turn out on to a surface lightly dusted with oatmeal and roll out until about 1 inch thick, then cut into triangles. Heat an ungreased griddle or frying pan and cook for about 4 to 5 minutes on each side until golden. Serve hot with butter.

Irish Johnny Cakes

These little honey cakes contain dried fruit and oatmeal and are delicious eaten freshly baked.

2 oz. flour	3 oz. honey
1½ teaspoons baking powder	1 tablespoon milk
6 oz. oatmeal	1 egg, beaten
3 oz. butter	2 oz. currants or sultanas

Set oven to 400ºF or Mark 6. Sift together into a bowl the flour and baking powder, stir in the oatmeal then rub in the butter. Warm the honey in a bowl set over a pan of hot water, then stir in to it the milk and beaten egg. Add the honey mixture to the oatmeal mixture, combining well. Add the dried fruit and stir lightly to distribute evenly. Using a spoon, place heaps of the mixture, approximately 2 inches apart, on a well-greased baking sheet and bake for 20 to 25 minutes. Cool on a wire rack and eat very fresh.

Steeplechasing

Apple Teabread

Apples have always been important in Ireland and not only for eating. They were considered a magical fruit and so were always served, in various forms, at Hallowe'en.

4 cooking apples, peeled, cored and grated	**8 oz. flour**
	6 oz. sugar
½ teaspoon finely grated lemon rind	**4 oz. butter**
	1 egg, beaten

Milk to mix

Set oven to 350ºF or Mark 4. Mix together the grated apple and lemon rind. Sift the flour into the sugar in a bowl, then rub in the butter until the mixture resembles breadcrumbs. Stir in the grated apple and beaten egg and mix well adding sufficient milk to make a smooth dough. Turn into a shallow, buttered 7 to 8 inch tin and smooth over the top. Bake for 35 to 40 minutes until golden brown. Test that it is fully cooked through by inserting a warm skewer; when this comes out clean, the teabread is cooked. Serve warm, spread with butter.

Apple Teabread is somewhat similar to Apple Brack, except that this recipe contains raisins and the apples are cooked before being added to the mixture.

Almond Cake

Almonds provided a flavouring that was especially popular in the 18th and 19th centuries and this deliciously light cake is an ideal accompaniment to tea, coffee or a glass of sherry or Madeira wine.

6 oz. butter	**5 oz. flour**
6 oz. caster sugar	**½ teaspoon baking powder**
3 large eggs, beaten	**3 oz. ground almonds**

A few drops almond or ratafia essence

Set oven to 400°F or Mark 6. Cream the butter and sugar together in a bowl until fluffy, then add the beaten eggs a little at a time, beating well between each addition. Sift together the flour and baking powder and fold into the mixture, together with the ground almonds and essence and mix to a soft, dropping consistency. Turn into a shallow, oblong baking tin lined with buttered greaseproof paper and bake for 20 to 25 minutes, until lightly golden and until a warm skewer inserted into the cake comes out clean. Turn out on to a wire rack and when cold cut into fingers or squares.

If desired, this cake can be iced before cutting up, with glacé or butter icing and decorated with flaked almonds.

Pulling for Home

Oaten Bread

Oats appear a great deal in Irish baking and Oaten Bread was widely eaten on a daily basis, with Wheaten Bread being reserved for high days and holidays.

4 oz. rolled oats
¼ pint buttermilk or sour milk
5 oz. flour
¼ teaspoon bicarbonate of soda
¼ teaspoon salt

Place the oats in a bowl, pour over the buttermilk, cover and leave to soak overnight in a cool place. Set oven to 350°F or Mark 4. Sift the flour, bicarbonate of soda and salt together and add to the soaked oats. Mix to a stiff dough, then knead until smooth. Turn out on to a lightly floured surface and divide in half. Roll each half into a round about 2½ inches thick. Place on a lightly greased baking sheet and bake for about 40 minutes or until well risen and golden brown. Serve warm, spread with butter.

Slim Cakes

These thin, quickly made cakes, traditionally baked on a griddle and popular for breakfast as well as tea, would be eaten at one sitting, as they are not 'keepers'.

8 oz. flour	**2 to 2½ oz. butter**
Pinch of salt	**1 egg, beaten**

Hot milk

Sift the flour and salt together into a bowl, then rub in the butter until the mixture resembles breadcrumbs. Add the beaten egg and sufficient hot milk to produce a smooth, elastic dough. Roll out on a lightly floured surface to about ½ inch thick, then cut into rounds. Heat a griddle or thick frying pan, butter lightly and cook the cakes for about 4 to 5 minutes on each side until golden. Serve warm.

Boiled Cake

Boiled fruit cakes are deliciously moist, good 'keepers' and very popular.

3 oz. golden syrup	4 oz. butter
4 oz. caster sugar	8 oz. flour
4 fluid oz. water or	½ teaspoon baking powder
cold tea (no milk)	1 teaspoon mixed spice
4 oz. currants	1 teaspoon ground ginger
4 oz. sultanas	1 egg, beaten

Boil the syrup, water or cold tea, sugar, fruit and butter together for 5 minutes, then allow to cool. Set oven to 350°F or Mark 4. Sift together the flour, baking powder and spices and fold into the boiled mixture, then add the egg and mix to a soft consistency. Turn into a greased and base-lined 7 inch cake tin and bake for 1½ to 2 hours, covering the top with a piece of kitchen foil if it appears to be browning too quickly. Cool in the tin for 5 minutes, then turn out on to a wire rack.

Irish Treacle Loaf

Black treacle is a popular flavouring for tealoaves and scones in Ireland and this loaf also contains both dried fruit and spice.

2 oz. butter	½ lb. flour
2½ fl. oz. water	½ teaspoon ground ginger
2 oz. black treacle	½ teaspoon ground mixed spice
2 oz. soft brown sugar	1 teaspoon bicarbonate of soda
1 egg, beaten	2 oz. currants
2 oz. raisins or sultanas	

Set oven to 350ºF or Mark 4. In a pan, melt the butter in the water. Mix together in a bowl the treacle, sugar and beaten egg. Sift together the flour, ginger, spice and bicarbonate of soda and add to the treacle mixture. Fold in the dried fruit and mix thoroughly, then stir in the butter and water mixture. Turn into one 2 lb. or two 1 lb. loaf tins, greased and base-lined and bake for 1¼ to 2 hours, covering the top with kitchen foil if it appears to be browning too quickly. Allow to cool in the tin for 5 minutes, then turn out on to a wire rack. Serve sliced, plain or with butter.

A Home in Donegal

Apple and Potato Cake

This autumn cake, originally baked on a griddle, was traditionally served at Hallowe'en, when a lucky ring would be hidden in the apple filling.

1 lb. potatoes, weighed after peeling
1 oz. melted butter
2 oz. flour or 1½ oz. flour and
** ½ oz. oatmeal combined**
Pinch of salt
2 teaspoons sugar

8 to 10 oz. cooking or dessert apples,
** peeled, cored and thinly sliced and**
** weighed after preparation**
A little milk
1 oz. butter, cut into flakes
1 oz. sugar, white or brown

Pinch of ground ginger or cinnamon

Boil the potatoes in water until tender. Drain *very* well, mash with the melted butter and allow to cool slightly. Set oven to 400ºF or Mark 6. Add the flour, salt and sugar to the mashed potato and knead to form a pliable dough. Divide in half and roll out each half on a lightly floured surface to form two rounds about ½ inch thick. Arrange the apple slices over one round and top with the other, sealing the edges. Place on a greased baking sheet, brush with a little milk and bake for 25 to 30 minutes until golden brown. Remove from the oven and carefully remove the top. Sprinkle the apple with butter flakes, sugar and spice, replace the top and return to the oven for a further 2 to 3 minutes. Serve at once, cut into slices.

Vicarage Cake

This eggless cake contains vinegar which, combined with the bicarbonate of soda and milk, gives it a light texture. Such cakes, often made when the hens were off lay, are ideal for anyone unable to eat eggs.

12 oz. flour	3 oz. currants
4 oz. butter	½ teaspoon bicarbonate of soda
4 oz. caster sugar	12 tablespoons milk
4 oz. sultanas	1½ tablespoons vinegar

Set oven to 350ºF or Mark 4. Sift the flour into a bowl, rub in the butter until the mixture resembles breadcrumbs, then stir in the sugar and dried fruit. Mix the bicarbonate of soda with 2 tablespoons of milk - it will froth slightly - then add the remainder of the milk and stir into the dry mixture with the vinegar. Mix well and turn into a greased and lined 8 inch cake tin. Bake for 1½ hours, covering the top with kitchen foil if it appears to be browning too quickly. Cool in the tin for 5 minutes, then turn out on to a wire rack.

A Home in Achill

Irish Shortcakes

Originally, these curranty biscuits were made with bacon fat.

8 oz. flour	**2 oz. caster sugar**
½ teaspoon baking powder	**3 oz. currants**
2 oz. lard	**1 small egg, beaten**

A little milk to mix

Set oven to 350°F or Mark 4. Sift the flour and baking powder together into a bowl then rub in the lard until the mixture resembles breadcrumbs. Stir in the sugar and currants and mix to a stiff dough with the beaten egg, adding a little milk if necessary. Roll out to about ½ inch thick on a lightly floured surface, cut into 2½ inch rounds or squares and place on a greased baking sheet. Prick with a fork and bake for about 30 minutes or until golden. Transfer to a wire rack to cool.

Boxty Bread

'Boxty on the griddle, Boxty in the pan; if you can't make Boxty, you'll never get a man'.
Boxty is a traditional potato bread from the Northern Counties of Ireland.

1½ lb potatoes, weighed after peeling	12 oz. self-raising flour
	1 teaspoon baking powder
Salt and white pepper	2 to 2¼ oz. butter, melted
Milk to mix	

Divide the potatoes in half and boil one half in salted water until tender. Grate the remaining half into a clean tea towel and wring out the liquid into a bowl, where the starch will gradually sink to the bottom. Drain the boiled potatoes well and mash, seasoning to taste. Mix the grated and mashed potato together, then sift in the flour and baking powder. Drain off the reserved liquid from the starch, add the starch to the potato mixture and mix well. Melt the butter, stir in and mix to a soft dough, adding a little milk if the mixture seems too dry. Set oven to 400°F or Mark 6. Turn the dough out on to a lightly floured surface and knead gently. Shape into four flat, round cakes and mark each with a cross. Brush with a little milk to glaze, place on a greased baking sheet and bake for 25 to 30 minutes, or until well risen and golden brown. Divide into quarters or 'farls' along the cross marks and serve warm with butter.

Boxty Bread can also be cooked on a griddle, allowing about 15 minutes each side.

Plum Cake

Despite its name, 'plum' cake does not contain plums at all, but is an appetising mixture of dried fruit and candied peel. In the 18th century, 'Plumb' or Heavy Cakes were not only exceedingly popular but also exceedingly rich and very large indeed!

8 oz. butter	**¼ teaspoon ground ginger**
8 oz. caster sugar	**3 oz. ground almonds**
5 eggs	**6 oz. raisins or sultanas**
8 oz. flour	**6 oz. currants**
¼ teaspoon ground cinnamon	**2 oz. chopped mixed peel**
	1 oz. flaked almonds

Set oven to 325ºF or Mark 3. Cream the butter and sugar together in a bowl until fluffy. Whisk the eggs in a bowl over a pan of hot water and beat into the butter mixture, a little at a time. Sift together the flour and spices and fold into the mixture, together with the ground almonds. Stir in the dried fruit, peel and flaked almonds. Turn the mixture into a greased and lined 10 inch round cake tin, smooth over the top, hollowing it *very* slightly in the centre and bake for 2 to 2½ hours, covering the top with kitchen foil if it appears to be browning too quickly. Cool in the tin for 10 minutes, then turn out on to a wire rack.

Currant Soda Scones

These scones are richly fruited with sultanas and peel as well as currants and, traditionally, a knife is used to stir the mixture.

8 oz. flour	**1 oz. caster sugar**
1 teaspoon bicarbonate of soda	**1½ oz. currants**
1 teaspoon cream of tartar	**1½ oz. sultanas**
½ teaspoon salt	**1 oz. chopped mixed peel**
1½ oz. lard	**Buttermilk**

Set oven to 425°F or Mark 7. Sift together into a bowl the flour, bicarbonate of soda, cream of tartar and salt, then rub in the lard until the mixture resembles breadcrumbs. Add the sugar, dried fruit and peel, combining with a knife, then add sufficient buttermilk, stirring with the knife, to form a soft dough. Turn out on to a lightly floured surface and, with the hands, divide into 2 inch rounds, each about ½ inch thick. Place on a lightly greased baking sheet and glaze with a little extra buttermilk. Bake for about 10 minutes or until well risen and golden. Serve warm or cold, either plain or with butter.

This mixture can also be formed into a large round, in which case it should be baked for about 20 to 25 minutes.

The Departure

Ginger Cake

Ginger has always been a very popular spice with Irish cooks.

2 to 2½ oz. butter	Pinch of salt
4 oz. brown sugar	4 teaspoons baking powder
2 eggs, beaten	1 teaspoon ground ginger
2 tablespoons treacle or syrup	½ teaspoon ground cinnamon
1 teaspoon grated lemon rind	¼ teaspoon ground nutmeg
8 oz. flour	8 fluid oz. boiling water

Set oven to 350ºF or Mark 4. Cream the butter and sugar together in a bowl until fluffy, add each egg alternately with the treacle, beating well after each addition, then stir in the lemon rind. Sift together the flour, salt, baking powder and spices and fold into the mixture, then add the boiling water and mix well. Turn into a greased, shallow 9 inch tin and bake for 40 to 45 minutes or until the cake is springy, yet firm to the touch. Cool in the tin for 5 minutes, then turn out on to a wire rack.

Girdle Scones

Made with buttermilk, these little scones were originally cooked on a griddle or girdle, but if made in large rounds with each marked into four quarters, they were known as Elcho Scones.

8 oz. flour	**½ teaspoon salt**
½ teaspoon bicarbonate of soda	**1½ oz. lard**
½ teaspoon cream of tartar	**¼ pint buttermilk**

Set oven to 425°F or Mark 7. Sift together into a bowl the flour, bicarbonate of soda, cream of tartar and salt, then rub in the lard until the mixture resembles breadcrumbs. Add the buttermilk and mix to a smooth dough, adding a little extra buttermilk if necessary. Turn out on to a lightly floured surface and knead lightly. With the hands, form into small, flat rounds about ½ inch thick, place on a lightly greased baking sheet and bake for 10 to 15 minutes until golden. Serve hot or cold with butter.

Girdle Scones can be transformed into Treacle Scones by adding ¼ teaspoon of ground mixed spice to the flour mixture and dissolving 1 to 2 tablespoons of treacle in the buttermilk before using.

Hospitality

Farmhouse Loaf

A teatime loaf containing fruit; a recipe which comes from County Donegal.

1½ to 2 oz. butter	½ level teaspoon mixed spice
4 oz. sugar	Grated rind of half a lemon
8 oz. flour	4 oz. currants
2 level teaspoons baking powder	4 oz. sultanas or raisins
Pinch of salt	1 large egg, beaten
Pinch of bicarbonate of soda	½ pint buttermilk

Set oven to 300°F or Mark 2. Cream the butter and sugar together in a bowl, then sift in the flour, baking powder, salt, bicarbonate of soda and spice. Mix well, then stir in the lemon rind and dried fruit. Add the beaten egg and buttermilk and mix to a very soft dough, adding a little extra flour if the mixture seems rather too slack. Turn into a buttered and base-lined 2 lb. loaf tin and bake for 1 to 1¼ hours until cooked through, covering the top with kitchen foil if it appears to be browning too quickly. Cool in the tin for 5 minutes, then turn out on to a wire rack. Serve sliced with butter.

Almond Shortbread

This rich shortbread was traditionally made for Christmas tea.

5 oz. flour	4 egg yolks, beaten
1 heaped tablespoon ground rice	1 egg white
2 heaped tablespoons sugar	4 oz. icing sugar
4 oz. butter	1½ to 2 oz. flaked almonds

Set oven to 300°F or Mark 2. Mix together in a bowl the flour, ground rice and sugar, then rub in the butter until the mixture resembles breadcrumbs. Add the egg yolks and mix to form a stiff dough. Knead until smooth, then roll out on a lightly floured surface to a size to fit a buttered 7 inch tin. Press in until flat, then prick with a fork. Cover with a piece of greaseproof paper or kitchen foil and bake for 25 to 30 minutes. Whisk the egg white until it stands up in soft peaks, then sift the icing sugar and fold in. Remove the shortbread from the oven, remove the covering and spread the icing mixture over the top. Sprinkle with the flaked almonds and return to the oven for a further 20 to 25 minutes. Cool in the tin and cut into wedges or fingers when cold.

Honey Cake

Honey has always been popular and, in a 10th-century Irish poem, it is referred to, along with apples, as one of the foods 'given by God'. This Honey Cake is plain, but in other recipes the ingredients can include mixed peel, almonds, spices and lemon.

4 oz. butter	2 eggs, beaten
1½ oz. soft brown sugar	6 oz. flour
2 tablespoons clear honey	1 teaspoon baking powder

3 to 4 tablespoons milk

Set oven to 350°F or Mark 4. Cream the butter, sugar and honey together in a bowl, then add the beaten eggs, a little at a time. Sift the flour and baking powder together and fold into the mixture. Stir in the milk, beat lightly and pour into a greased and lined 7 inch cake tin. Bake for 40 to 45 minutes until the cake is springy to the touch. Cool on a wire rack. This cake keeps well.

Carvie Cake

This is the Irish country name for Seed Cake; a cake that has been popular since the 18th century and has never really gone out of favour.

8 oz. butter, softened	8 oz. self-raising flour
8 oz. caster sugar	1 heaped tablespoon caraway seeds
4 eggs	3 tablespoons milk

Set oven to 325°F or Mark 3. Cream the butter and sugar together in a bowl until fluffy, then beat in the eggs, one at a time, adding a little flour with each addition. Fold in the remaining flour and the caraway seeds, then stir in the milk. Turn into a greased and lined 8 inch cake tin and bake for 1½ to 1¾ hours, covering the top with kitchen foil if it appears to be browning too quickly. Cool in the tin for 10 minutes, then turn out on to a wire rack.

Washing Day in the West

Apple Cheesecakes

Served warm, these little cheesecakes have an apple filling and are topped with a macaroon-like almond mixture.

8 oz. prepared sweet shortcrust pastry (ideally made with butter)
4 oz. caster sugar
3 oz. ground almonds
¼ oz. ground rice
The *unbeaten* white of 1 large egg
(if the egg is small, a second white may be required)

A few drops of vanilla essence
4 oz. apple pulp, sieved and weighed after preparation
1 teaspoon melted butter
2½ oz. Madeira or sponge cake crumbs
Sifted icing sugar for dusting

Set oven to 350°F or Mark 4. Roll out the pastry on a lightly floured surface and use to line 10 to 12 greased and floured tartlet tins. Mix the sugar, ground almonds and ground rice together in a bowl with the unbeaten egg white and vanilla essence, then set aside. Mix the apple pulp with the melted butter and the cake crumbs, divide between the tartlet tins and top with the almond mixture. Bake for 25 minutes until golden. Remove from the tartlet tins and serve warm, dusted thickly with sifted icing sugar.

Spice Bread

This moist teabread improves with keeping and was originally stored wrapped in a cloth.

10 oz. flour	4 oz. light brown sugar
1 teaspoon baking powder	6 oz. sultanas
Pinch of salt	1 oz. chopped mixed peel
1 teaspoon mixed spice	4 oz. golden syrup
$1/4$ teaspoon ground ginger	2 oz. butter
$1/4$ teaspoon nutmeg or cinnamon	1 egg, beaten
Grated rind of half a lemon	3 to 4 tablespoons milk

Set oven to 350ºF or Mark 4. Sift together into a bowl the flour, baking powder, salt and spices, then stir in the lemon rind, sugar, sultanas and peel. Warm the syrup and butter together in a pan, then stir into the mixture with the beaten egg and milk, combining thoroughly. Turn into a greased and base-lined 2 lb. loaf tin, smooth over the top and bake for 30 minutes, then reduce the temperature to 325ºF or Mark 3 and bake for a further 40 to 45 minutes, covering the top with kitchen foil if it appears to be browning too quickly. Test with a warm skewer at the end of baking time; the skewer will come out clean when the teabread is cooked. Cool in the tin for 10 minutes, then turn out on to a wire rack. Serve sliced with butter.

Refreshment for Man and Beast

Porter Cake

Porter was a type of stout widely used all over the British Isles for cooking, as well as drinking, and was sometimes known as 'the working man's pint'. In Ireland, Guinness, first brewed in 1759 in Dublin, is now usually used when making this rich fruit cake.

4 oz. butter	1 teaspoon mixed spice
4 oz. soft brown sugar	¼ pint Guinness
2 eggs, lightly beaten	6 oz. raisins
8 oz. flour	6 oz. sultanas
½ teaspoon baking powder	Finely grated rind of a lemon

Set oven to 325°F or Mark 3. Cream the butter and sugar together in a bowl until fluffy, then beat in the eggs, a little at a time. Sift together the flour, baking powder and spice and fold into the mixture. Add the Guinness, beating well, then stir in the fruit and lemon rind and turn the mixture into a greased and lined 7 inch tin. Bake for 1½ hours, covering the top with kitchen foil if it appears to be browning too quickly. Allow to cool completely in the tin, then wrap in greaseproof paper and kitchen foil and store for a week to ten days before eating.

If desired, this cake can be fed halfway through storing time with a little extra Guinness. Unwrap the cake, pierce a few holes in its base with a fine skewer and pour over a dessertspoon of Guinness. Leave for 40 minutes before rewrapping.

Belem Tarts

These rich tartlets, with their filling of egg yolks and cream, are deliciously extravagant and a special teatime treat.

4 to 5 oz. prepared flaky pastry   **4 oz. caster sugar**
5 egg yolks   **½ pint double cream**
Pinch of salt   **Ground cinnamon**

Set oven to 400°F or Mark 6. Roll out the pastry on a lightly floured surface and use to line 8 to 10 lightly buttered and floured tartlet tins. Whisk the egg yolks together in a bowl with the salt, then beat in the sugar and cream. Spoon the filling into the pastry cases and sprinkle over the ground cinnamon. Bake for about 20 minutes until the filling is set and golden. Cool on a wire rack.

Irish Rink Cake

A light, buttery cake topped with almonds and currants.

4 oz. flour	**4 oz. caster sugar**
½ teaspoon baking powder	**2 eggs, beaten**
2 oz. butter, softened	**1 oz. currants**

2 oz. blanched, chopped almonds

Set oven to 350ºF or Mark 4. Sift the flour and baking powder together into a bowl, then rub in the butter until the mixture resembles breadcrumbs. Add the sugar, then mix to a dropping consistency with the beaten eggs, adding them a little at a time. Turn into a greased and base-lined 8 inch sandwich tin. Mix the currants and almonds together and sprinkle evenly over the top of the cake. Bake for about 20 minutes or until springy to the touch. Cool in the tin for 5 minutes, then turn out on to a wire rack.

METRIC CONVERSIONS

The weights, measures and oven temperatures used in the preceding recipes can be easily converted to their metric equivalents. The conversions listed below are only approximate, having been rounded up or down as may be appropriate.

Weights

Avoirdupois	Metric
1 oz.	just under 30 grams
4 oz. (¼ lb.)	app. 115 grams
8 oz. (½ lb.)	app. 230 grams
1 lb.	454 grams

Liquid Measures

Imperial	Metric
1 tablespoon (liquid only)	20 millilitres
1 fl. oz.	app. 30 millilitres
1 gill (¼ pt.)	app. 145 millilitres
½ pt.	app. 285 millilitres
1 pt.	app. 570 millilitres
1 qt.	app. 1.140 litres

Oven Temperatures

	°Fahrenheit	Gas Mark	°Celsius
Slow	300	2	150
	325	3	170
Moderate	350	4	180
	375	5	190
	400	6	200
Hot	425	7	220
	450	8	230
	475	9	240

Flour as specified in these recipes refers to plain flour unless otherwise described.